Nobel Prize
Winners

This book is to be r~
he last date stamp~ ~ Hacke
ch

1   ~009

2'

Crabtree Publishing Company

Dedication

This series is dedicated to every woman who has followed her dreams and to every young girl who hopes to do the same. While overcoming great odds and often oppression, the remarkable women in this series have triumphed in their fields. Their dedication, hard work, and excellence can serve as an inspiration to all—young and old, male and female. Women in Profile *is both an acknowledgment of and a tribute to these great women.*

Project Manager
Lauri Seidlitz
Crabtree Editor
Virginia Mainprize
Copy Editors
Krista McLuskey
Leslie Strudwick
Design and Layout
Warren Clark

Published by Crabtree Publishing Company

350 Fifth Avenue, Suite 3308
New York, NY
USA 10018

360 York Road, R.R. 4
Niagara-on-the-Lake
Ontario, Canada
L0S 1J0

Cataloging-in-Publication Data

Hacker, Carlotta.
    Nobel Prize winners / Carlotta Hacker.
         p. cm. — (Women in profile)
    Includes bibliographical references and index.
    Summary: Chronicles the lives and achievements of women who have received Nobel Prizes in a variety of fields, including Aung San Suu Kyi, Barbara McClintock, and Nadine Gordimer.
    ISBN 0-7787-0007-0. — ISBN 0-7787-0029-1 (pbk.)
    1. Nobel Prizes—Biography—Juvenile literature. 2. Women scientists—Biography—Juvenile literature. 3. Women pacifists—Biography—Juvenile literature. 4. Women authors—Biography—Juvenile literature. [1. Nobel Prizes. 2. Women—Biography.] I. Title II. Series.
AS911.N9H29 1998   97-53222
001.4'4—dc21   CIP
                                        AC

Photograph Credits
Every reasonable effort has been made to trace ownership and to obtain permission to reprint copyright material. The publishers would be pleased to have any errors or omissions brought to their attention so that they may be corrected in subsequent printings.
Agence France Presse/Corbis-Bettmann: page 45; Archive Photos: cover, pages 6, 10, 13, 16, 17, 34, 36, 39; Canapress Photo Service: page 26; Corbis: page 15; Corbis-Bettmann: pages 12, 14; Farrar, Straus & Giroux: page 20 (Jerry Bauer); Globe Photos, Inc.: pages 30 (Andrea Renault), 35 (Walter Weismann); Marcus Rhoades: page 25; The Nobel Foundation: pages 7, 28, 32, 38; Photofest: page 31, 42; Reuters/Corbis-Bettmann: pages 9 (David Brunnnstom Stringer), 18, 22 (Mark Cardwell), 23 (Juda Ngwenya), 41 (Arthur Tsang), 21; Topham Picture Point: page 11; UPI/Corbis-Bettmann: pages 24, 27, 29, 33, 40, 43, 44.

Contents

6
Aung San Suu Kyi
Burmese Politician

12
Marie Curie
Polish Physicist

18
Nadine Gordimer
South African Writer

24
Barbara McClintock
American Geneticist

30
Toni Morrison
American Writer

36
Mairead Corrigan and Betty Williams
Irish Peace Activists

More Women in Profile

Laura Jane Addams   42
American Social Worker

Emily Greene Balch   42
American Peace Activist

Gerty Radnitz Cori   42
Czechoslovakian Biochemist

Gertrude Elion   42
American Biochemist

Maria Goeppert-Mayer   43
German Physicist

Dorothy Crowfoot Hodgkin   43
English Chemist and Crystallographer

Irène Joliot-Curie   43
French Radiochemist

Rita Levi-Montalcini   43
Italian Neuroembryologist

Gabriela Mistral   44
Chilean Poet

Leonie Nelly Sachs   44
German Writer and Holocaust Survivor

Bertha von Suttner   44
Austrian Author and Pacifist

Mother Teresa   45
Yugoslavian Missionary Nun

Jody Williams   45
American Anti-war Activist

Rosalyn Sussman Yalow   45
American Medical Physicist

Glossary   46

Suggested Reading   47

Index   48

Nobel Prize Winners

T he Nobel Prize owes its origins to Alfred Nobel, a Swedish scientist. Born in 1833, he manufactured explosives, including dynamite, which he invented in 1866. The invention made him rich.

As the years passed, Alfred became unhappy that his products were being used to kill people. Many of his friends were **pacifists** trying to put a stop to war. Alfred began to wish that he, too, could do something to make the world more peaceful.

Alfred never married, so he had no children to whom he could leave his fortune. In 1893, he decided to put aside money for a prize that would go to a person who had worked for the cause of peace. By the time Alfred died in 1896, he had created five prizes that were to be awarded each year. Prizes were to be given for peace, **chemistry**, **physics**, **physiology** and medicine, and literature. Those who win receive a medal and a cash award. In 1969, a sixth prize for **economics** was set up by the Swedish Central Bank.

Several committees decide who will receive the awards. The committee members come from the Swedish Academy of Science and other organizations.

Women were prize winners almost from the beginning. One of the first people to win the Nobel Peace Prize was Bertha von Suttner, a pacifist who had been a strong influence on Alfred. She received the award in 1905. Another early prize winner was Marie Curie, who received the Nobel Prize in physics in 1903.

Nevertheless, few women received the prizes in the early days. This was because there were few women scientists, and the Nobel committee seldom heard about them. The most common prizes given to women were usually for literature or peace. Even women who did exceptional work in the sciences were often overlooked—except for Marie Curie, who had become famous throughout the world.

In recent years, things have changed. Many more women are receiving the award in all fields. This book tells you about some of these women and their accomplishments.

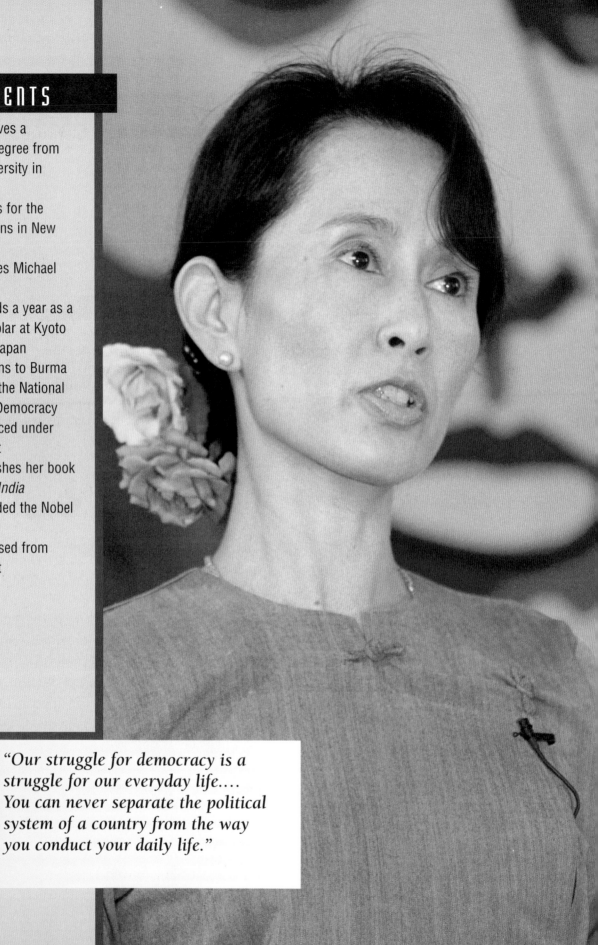

KEY EVENTS

1967 Receives a bachelor's degree from Oxford University in England

1969 Works for the United Nations in New York

1972 Marries Michael Aris

1985 Spends a year as a visiting scholar at Kyoto University, Japan

1988 Returns to Burma and founds the National League for Democracy

1989 Is placed under house arrest

1990 Publishes her book *Burma and India*

1991 Awarded the Nobel Peace Prize

1995 Released from house arrest

"Our struggle for democracy is a struggle for our everyday life.... You can never separate the political system of a country from the way you conduct your daily life."

Aung San Suu Kyi

Burmese Politician

Early Years

Suu Kyi was born in Rangoon, the capital city of Burma. Although her father died when she was two, she grew up under his shadow. Her family was important in Burmese politics, and her father was a national hero.

When Suu Kyi was fifteen, her mother became the Burmese ambassador to India. Suu Kyi went with her, and there she learned about India's national hero, Mohandas Gandhi. Like Suu Kyi's father, Gandhi had worked for freedom and justice for his people. He and his followers believed in peaceful protest and did not use violence even when they were attacked. These ideas made a great impression on Suu Kyi.

BACKGROUNDER

General Aung San

Suu Kyi's father, General Aung San, was one of Burma's greatest heroes. People called him *Bogyoke* which means "great general." As a student in the 1930s, he led the movement that was trying to free Burma from British rule. After World War II, Aung San formed a political party to work for Burmese **independence**. The British agreed to leave and arranged for free elections. Aung San's party won, but he was **assassinated** by his enemies before he could become prime minister. He was only thirty-two years old.

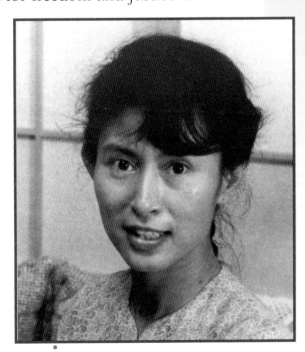

Like Mohandas Gandhi, Suu Kyi rejects the use of violence.

BACKGROUNDER

Burma (Myanmar)

Almost a thousand years ago, Burma was an independent kingdom. Later, it was conquered by other nations. In the nineteenth century, it became part of the British Empire and was ruled by Britain. During World War II, Japan conquered Burma. The Burmese people hated Japanese rule even more than British rule. After Japan's defeat, the British again ruled Burma for a few years, but in 1948, Burma became an independent country. It was run as a **democracy** until 1962 when a group of army officers seized power. Since then, Burma has been ruled by a military council that allows no opposition. The country's name was changed to Myanmar in 1989.

Developing Skills

Suu Kyi was in India when the Burmese army took over the government in 1962. She did not return home. She went to England and enrolled at Oxford University where she studied politics, philosophy, and **economics**. She would have liked to study English literature, but she chose subjects that would train her to help her country. Suu Kyi hoped to return home one day.

After getting her bachelor's degree, Suu Kyi taught in England. Then she moved to New York City where she worked for the United Nations. In 1972, she married Michael Aris whom she had met at Oxford. Before they married, Suu Kyi asked him to promise that he would not stand in her way if she ever needed to go back to Burma. Michael promised.

During the next few years, the couple lived in Oxford where Michael was a specialist in Tibetan studies. During the mid-1980s, while Michael was working in India, Suu Kyi went to Japan to do research on her father's life. The more Suu Kyi learned about her father, the more she began to feel that she should help her country.

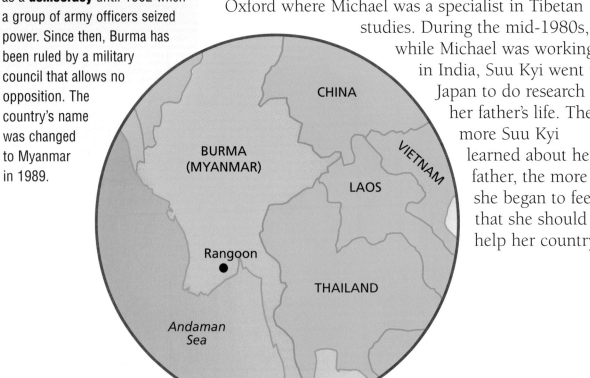

CHINA

BURMA (MYANMAR)

VIETNAM

LAOS

Rangoon

THAILAND

Andaman Sea

In 1988, Suu Kyi went home to Burma to care for her dying mother. The country was in turmoil. After twenty-six years of military rule, Burma had become one of the poorest countries in Asia. The people were so desperate that they were risking their lives to challenge the government.

Things reached a peak that year when thousands of students marched through the streets. They demanded free elections and the right to choose their leaders. The students were met with bullets as soldiers and police fired into the crowds. This led to more demonstrations—and more deaths. In August 1988, more than three thousand people were killed in one week.

Suu Kyi could not stand by and do nothing. "As my father's daughter, I felt I had a duty to get involved," she said.

During a traditional new year ceremony, Suu Kyi sprinkles water over the heads of her supporters.

"It was only when I grew older and started collecting material on my father's life that I began to learn ... how much he had achieved in his thirty-two years."

BACKGROUNDER

A Person of Great Courage

In taking a strong stand against the military government, Suu Kyi knew her life was in danger. In 1989, the government ordered soldiers to kill her at a political meeting. When Suu Kyi saw the soldiers taking aim, she quietly walked toward them, asking the crowd to move aside. The officer in charge was so impressed with Suu Kyi's courage that he ordered the soldiers not to shoot. Suu Kyi later explained that she had wanted to present the soldiers with a single target. She did not want anyone else to get shot.

Accomplishments

Suu Kyi made her first important speech in August 1988. At Burma's most sacred shrine, Shwedagon Pagoda, she spoke of her country's need for human rights, especially the right to choose its own government. The following month, she helped form the National League for Democracy (NLD). Suu Kyi traveled throughout the country, speaking in cities and tiny villages.

Whenever Suu Kyi spoke, huge crowds gathered to hear her. The soldiers did not dare attack so many people, but they tried to frighten Suu Kyi's supporters. When these efforts failed, the military government promised that it would hold elections in 1990.

It looked as if Suu Kyi had won her fight for democracy. However, in 1989, the government placed her under house arrest so she could not campaign in the elections. Despite this, her party won eighty percent of the vote. Suu Kyi should have become the leader of the country, but the military rulers did not want to give up power. They kept Suu Kyi locked in her house, and they arrested her closest supporters.

"The people of Burma are like prisoners in their own country, deprived of all freedom under military rule."

In 1991, Suu Kyi was awarded the Nobel Peace Prize "for her non-violent struggle for democracy and human rights." From the very beginning, she had followed Mohandas Gandhi's example and told her followers not to use violence, however much they were attacked. The Nobel committee called her struggle for democracy "one of the most extraordinary examples of civil courage in Asia in recent decades."

Suu Kyi's house arrest was ended in 1995, but she still has very little freedom. When her NLD party planned to hold a meeting after her release, the government arrested hundreds of party members.

In 1997, Suu Kyi secretly sent a videotape out of the country, calling on people throughout the world to help her bring democracy to Burma. She says she will not give up the fight until she has won her country's "second struggle for independence."

Quick Notes

- Suu Kyi is pronounced Soo Chee.

- Suu Kyi's name means "a bright collection of strange victories."

- Like most Burmese, Suu Kyi practices the Buddhist religion.

- Suu Kyi has two sons. During most of her house arrest, neither they nor their father were allowed to contact her.

- Suu Kyi's speeches, writings, and interviews have been published in several books, including *Freedom from Fear and Other Writings* (1991) and *The Voice of Hope* (1997).

A prisoner of conscience is someone who is put in jail because of his or her political beliefs.

KEY EVENTS

1891 Enrolls at the University of Paris
1893 Receives a master's degree in physics
1894 Receives a master's degree in mathematics
1895 Marries Pierre Curie
1898 Discovers polonium and radium
1903 Awarded the Nobel Prize in physics
1906 Appointed professor at the University of Paris
1911 Awarded the Nobel Prize in chemistry
1921 Visits the United States for the first time

"I believe that science has great beauty. A scientist in his laboratory is not a mere technician; he is also a child confronting natural phenomena that impress him as though they were fairy tales."

Marie Curie

Polish Physicist

Early Years

Marie grew up in the city of Warsaw while it was part of the Russian Empire. Both of her parents were teachers. Her mother, Bronislawa Sklodowska, was principal of a girls school. Her father, Vladislav, taught **physics** and math in a local school until he was replaced by a Russian teacher.

After Marie's father was fired, he began to take in boarding students and teach them. This made the family apartment very crowded. Marie gave up her bedroom and slept beside the dining room table.

Things became even worse when Marie's mother died. Marie was eleven, and she missed her mother. Even so, she did not fall behind with her schoolwork. Her father told her it was important for Poles to get a good education. Marie was proud of being Polish, and she worked so hard that she graduated top of her class.

BACKGROUNDER

Poland under Russian Rule

In the late eighteenth century, Russia, Austria, and Prussia (Germany) took over Poland and divided it among themselves. Marie grew up in the region taken over by Russia. Children had to speak Russian at school and were punished if they spoke Polish. Some Poles tried to **rebel** against the Russian Empire. Others kept their nationality strong by secretly teaching their children about Polish history and culture.

Marie's father taught her to believe in the importance of a good education.

Developing Skills

Marie and her older sister, Bronya, both wanted to go to college. Bronya hoped to study medicine, and Marie wanted to specialize in science. Their brother was a student at the University of Warsaw, but they knew they could not go there. Universities in the Russian Empire did not accept women.

"It was like a new world opened to me, the world of science, which I was at last permitted to know."

The sisters decided that they would study in France, taking turns so that they could pay for each other's tuition. First, Marie would get a job while Bronya was at medical school in Paris. Afterwards,

Bronya would support Marie's studies at the University of Paris. But Marie hated the only job she could get. For six years, she worked as a governess for a rich Polish family who lived far from Warsaw and treated her as a servant.

At last, in 1891, Marie enrolled at the University of Paris. She had very little money. She rented an attic room without heat or electricity, but she was happy. She did so well in her studies that she was at the top of her class when she received her master's degree in physics in 1893. The next year, she was second in her class when she got her master's degree in mathematics.

In 1895, Marie married a French scientist called Pierre Curie. Two years later, after their daughter Irène was born, Marie began to work for her doctoral degree. As her research project, she chose to study uranium **atoms**. She wanted to find out why uranium rocks gave off mysterious waves or rays. She called these waves "**radiation**."

Within two months, Marie discovered two important things. First, she found that the strength of radiation depends on the amount of uranium in a piece of rock. Second, whatever she did to the uranium, the strength of the rays stayed the same. For example, whether she heated the uranium or mixed it with other substances, the amount of radiation did not change.

Marie suspected that radiation must be caused by movement inside the uranium atoms. She called this "radioactivity."

BACKGROUNDER

Chemical Elements

An element is a basic substance that cannot be broken down into simpler elements. This is because each element is composed of only one type of atom. Scientists have identified more than one hundred elements. They include aluminum, carbon, copper, gold, iron, and oxygen. Some elements are **radioactive**; for example, radium, polonium, thorium, and uranium.

Marie's discovery of radiation was a scientific breakthrough.

BACKGROUNDER

Radium

Radium glows with a bluish light. It also gives off heat. A piece of radium the size of a penny will produce about five hundred **calories** of heat every day for one thousand years. Radium is used to treat cancer, but it can be harmful if it is not handled carefully. Pierre and Marie had no idea it was dangerous. Pierre always carried a test tube of radium in his pocket to show to friends. Marie slept with some radium glowing by her bedside. Everything in the shed where they worked became radioactive. Even today, their notebooks are still dangerously radioactive. Marie and Pierre were affected, too. They were often tired and showed other signs of **radiation sickness**. Marie died of leukemia because of her work with radium.

"It was in this miserable old shed that the best and happiest years of our life were spent, entirely consecrated to work."

Accomplishments

During her experiments, Marie had found that another element, called thorium, was also radioactive. Her next step was to study minerals that contained thorium and uranium. To her surprise, she found that two types of minerals, pitchblende and chalcolite, were far more radioactive than she would have expected from the amount of uranium and thorium in them. What could be causing all this radioactivity?

Pierre Curie became so interested in this problem that he decided to join his wife in her research. Through their experiments, they discovered that the radiation was caused by two previously unknown elements. They named these elements polonium and radium. The most powerful was radium. It was one million times more radioactive than uranium.

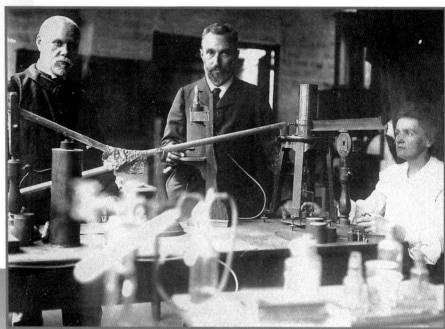

Marie and Pierre now began an enormous task. They had to separate the radium from the pitchblende in which it was found. This meant breaking up tons of rock to get just a few grains of radium. They did this in an old shed near Pierre's laboratory. It took them four years. Not until 1902 did they have enough radium—0.00035 ounces (0.1 grams)—to prove for certain that it existed.

In 1903, Marie wrote a paper describing her work. That same year, she and Pierre were awarded the Nobel Prize in physics "for their joint researches on radiation." The award was not given for their discovery of radium because that work was considered to deserve a separate prize. This was awarded to Marie in 1911 when she received the Nobel Prize in **chemistry**.

Marie continued to do further research on radium. She did most of it without Pierre, who had been killed in 1906 by a horse-drawn wagon. After his death, Marie was given a job at the University of Paris. She was the university's first woman professor.

As one of the world's most famous scientists, Marie received many awards and honors during her final years. She is still greatly honored today. Not only did she discover radium, but she also launched a new field of study—atomic physics. She opened up the tiny world inside the atom.

Quick Notes

- For sixty-one years, Marie was the only person who had won two Nobel Prizes in science.

- Marie never forgot that she was Polish. She taught her daughters to speak Polish, and she raised money to help train Polish scientists.

- She named polonium in honor of her Polish homeland.

- During World War I, Marie was head of two laboratories, one in Warsaw and one in Paris.

Marie's daughter Irène continued her mother's important studies with radioactivity. Irène won the Nobel Prize in chemistry in 1935.

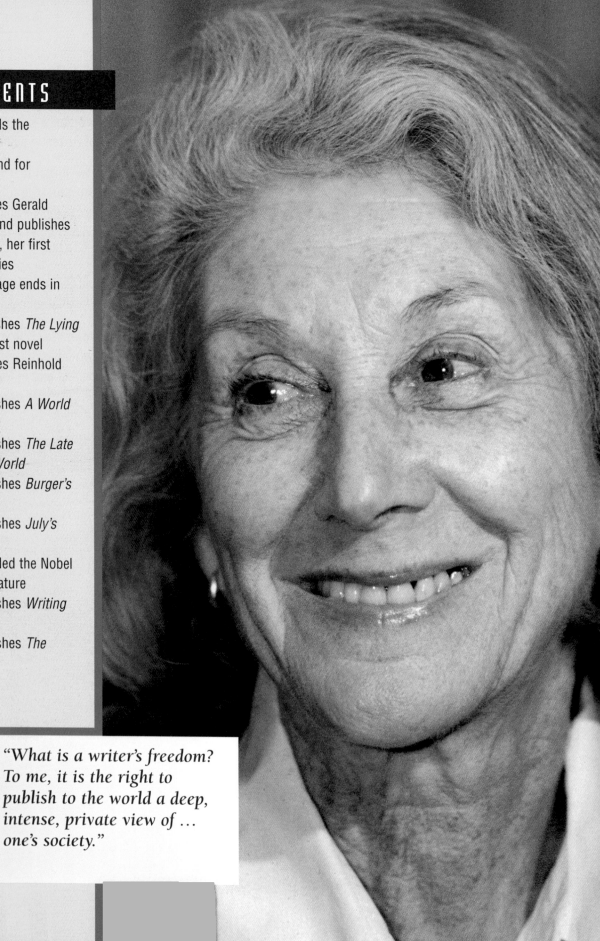

KEY EVENTS

1945 Attends the University of Witwatersrand for one year

1949 Marries Gerald Gavronsky and publishes *Face to Face*, her first book of stories

1952 Marriage ends in divorce

1953 Publishes *The Lying Days*, her first novel

1954 Marries Reinhold Cassirer

1958 Publishes *A World of Strangers*

1966 Publishes *The Late Bourgeois World*

1979 Publishes *Burger's Daughter*

1981 Publishes *July's People*

1991 Awarded the Nobel Prize in literature

1996 Publishes *Writing and Being*

1998 Publishes *The House Gun*

"What is a writer's freedom? To me, it is the right to publish to the world a deep, intense, private view of … one's society."

Nadine Gordimer
South African Writer

Early Years

When Nadine was nine, all the students in her class were told to write a poem. She wrote one about a famous South African leader. It began, "Noble in heart, Noble in mind, Never deceitful, Never unkind." Nadine enjoyed the rhythm so much that she decided to write more poetry. Before long, she was also writing stories.

Nadine lived in Springs, a small gold-mining town close to the city of Johannesburg in South Africa. When she was thirteen, she sent one of her stories to a Johannesburg newspaper. To her delight, it was published in the children's section. From then on, Nadine often wrote stories for the children's section of the paper.

As her stories became more mature, she sent them to magazines that were not just for children. Nadine was now competing with adult writers. She was thrilled when *Forum* magazine accepted one of her stories. She was fifteen at the time.

BACKGROUNDER

Nadine's Family

Nadine's parents were both Jewish immigrants to South Africa. Her father, Isidore Gordimer, was a watchmaker and jeweler from Lithuania. Her mother, Nan Meyer Gordimer, was from England. Nadine has an older sister named Betty.

BACKGROUNDER

Apartheid

Apartheid, which means separateness, was a South African system of racial laws. It was a policy in South Africa from 1948 to 1991. Under apartheid, people were divided into four races: black, white, Asian, and colored. Colored meant a person had parents from more than one race. Races had to live in separate areas. People were not allowed to marry or even date someone of another race. Races had separate schools, restaurants, buses, and even park benches. The system was particularly hard on black South Africans, who made up more than seventy percent of the population. They worked mainly at laboring jobs or as servants. They always had to carry a passbook saying who they were and where they were allowed to be.

Developing Skills

Nadine once said that she was brought up "on the soft side of the color-bar." She meant that things were easy for her because she was white. At the time, South Africa was organized under the system of apartheid which tried to keep black and white people separate. All the girls in Nadine's school were white, and so were all her neighbors.

Because Nadine read a lot as a teenager, she developed a different outlook from many of her neighbors. She saw that there were "all colors and kinds of people" in her country, yet she was not able to be friends with some of them. She could treat them as servants, but not as equals.

Nadine began to express her thoughts about the unfairness of apartheid in her stories. At first, the stories were printed only in South African publications. Then a friend encouraged her to send her work to other countries as well. Soon, her stories were appearing in the *New Yorker* and other well-known magazines.

"I have no political dogma—only plenty of doubts about everything except my conviction that the color-bar is wrong and utterly indefensible."

In 1949, Nadine gathered together a number of her stories and published them as a book. Three years later, she published a second collection. Meanwhile, she was busy writing a novel. It was about the racial **bigotry** of white people in a small community.

This first novel, which was called *The Lying Days*, set the tone for Nadine's later works. All her books deal with apartheid in a personal way. Nadine writes about the way apartheid affects people's private lives and harms their relationships with one another.

Since Nadine did not seem to be attacking the government, her books were allowed to be published. But as conditions in South Africa grew worse, she began to write more openly against apartheid. This brought her greater success and fame in other countries but did not please her own government.

In 1986, Nadine visited Alexandra, a black town near Johannesburg, to lay wreaths at the graves of political activists.

Accomplishments

Nadine's second novel, *A World of Strangers*, is about an English visitor who tries to be friends with both white and black South Africans. It was published in 1958 without problems, but the government decided to ban the paperback edition. When Nadine asked why the book had been banned, she was told that it "undermined the traditional race policy" of the country.

Two later books were also banned: *The Late Bourgeois World* (1966) and *Burger's Daughter* (1979). They were two of Nadine's most popular novels, yet South Africans were not allowed to read them.

These setbacks did not slow down Nadine's writing. She continued to produce both short stories and novels. Meanwhile, she protested against apartheid whenever she could. She also spoke against the censorship laws which were especially hard on black writers. Black South Africans were punished far more severely than white writers if the government disliked what they wrote. Nadine might have her books banned, but blacks could be sent to prison.

Nadine at a 1991 news conference in New York City.

"Censored, banned, gagged—the writers of my country are well on the way to becoming a victimized group."

Some black authors were so discouraged that they hardly wrote. To encourage them to keep writing, Nadine helped found the Congress of South African Writers in 1987. Most of its members were black.

By this time, Nadine was famous throughout the world, both for her stand against apartheid and for her books about life in South Africa. Recognized as one of the world's greatest writers, she was awarded the Nobel Prize in literature in 1991. She was the first South African to be honored with the prize.

When Nadine heard she had won the prize, she said that it was the second-best thing that had happened to her recently. The best thing had been the release from prison of the South African leader Nelson Mandela. His release led to the end of apartheid and a change of government in South Africa.

In the new South Africa, Nadine has continued to write about things that matter to her country. She finishes a novel every few years. Since she first began to write at the age of nine, she has written more than ten novels, as well as hundreds of short stories and articles.

Quick Notes

- In 1976, a South African newspaper chose Nadine as Woman of the Year. She refused the honor. She said it should go to one of the many black women who were fighting against apartheid.

- Nadine has won many awards, including the United Kingdom's Booker Prize.

- Nadine has been married twice and has one daughter and one son.

Nadine with Archbishop Desmond Tutu in 1991. Tutu won the Nobel Peace Prize in 1984.

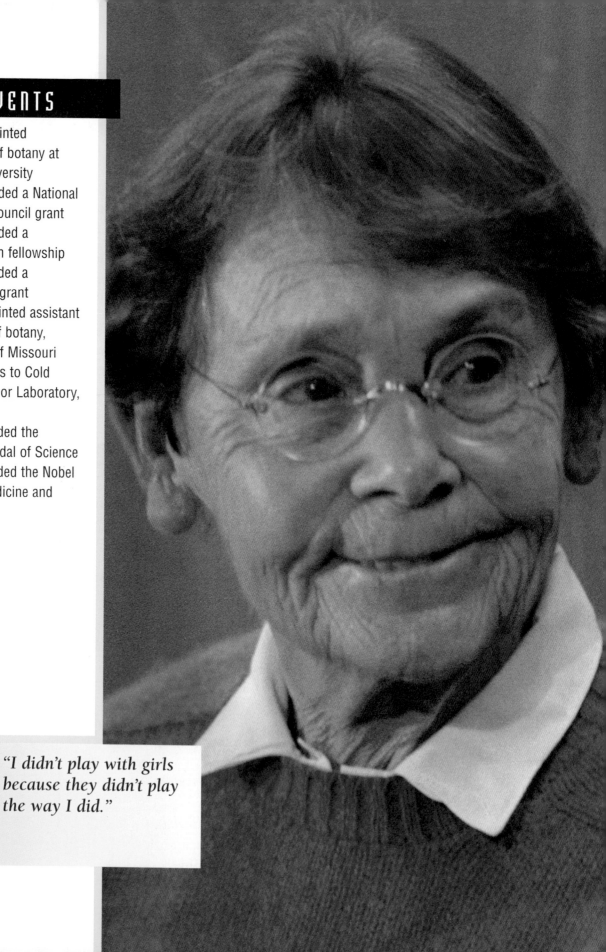

KEY EVENTS

1927 Appointed instructor of botany at Cornell University

1931 Awarded a National Research Council grant

1933 Awarded a Guggenheim fellowship

1934 Awarded a Rockefeller grant

1936 Appointed assistant professor of botany, University of Missouri

1941 Moves to Cold Spring Harbor Laboratory, Long Island

1970 Awarded the National Medal of Science

1983 Awarded the Nobel Prize in medicine and physiology

"I didn't play with girls because they didn't play the way I did."

Barbara McClintock

American Geneticist

Early Years

Barbara was a bundle of energy from a very young age. Her parents were going to call her Eleanor, but they thought the name seemed too calm for their lively baby. They decided the name Barbara suited her better.

Barbara was born in Hartford, Connecticut, but grew up in Brooklyn, New York. Her father was a doctor, and he encouraged his children to be active. There were four children in the family, three girls and a boy. Barbara was by far the most adventurous. She was always on the move—skating, bicycling, or playing baseball with the boys in her neighborhood.

When Barbara graduated from high school, she wanted to go to university, but her mother would not let her. Her mother thought higher education was bad for girls. Barbara's father would have let her go, but he was in France, serving in the army in World War I. When he returned home after the war, Barbara enrolled at Cornell University.

BACKGROUNDER

A Practical Person

When Barbara was about ten years old, an uncle showed her how to fix machinery. From then on, she repaired almost everything herself. At the laboratory, she cleaned and put together her microscopes. She always serviced her car rather than taking it to a garage. When she was eighty, she still changed the tires by herself.

Barbara with a group of scientists at Cornell University in 1929.

Developing Skills

Barbara loved Cornell from the moment she arrived. She joined its College of Agriculture and was soon absorbed in her work. After finishing her bachelor's degree in 1923, she stayed on to do graduate work.

Barbara decided to study genetics, the branch of **biology** that looks at how **characteristics** are passed from one generation to the next. The Cornell geneticists were doing this by studying corn. They had chosen corn because it was easy to see what changes were taking place from generation to generation. They could see that one corncob had more kernels than another or that some of the kernels were a different color. Even so, none of the geneticists had done a careful study of corn chromosomes.

Barbara made chromosomes her speciality. She cut corn kernels into thin slices and studied them under a microscope. The chromosomes were big enough for her to see, although she could not see the genes on them. However, by doing experiments with the chromosomes, she figured out how the genes were arranged.

Barbara working at her Cold Spring Harbor Laboratory in 1947. Her work was almost unrecognized until she won the Nobel Prize.

After receiving her doctorate, Barbara stayed at Cornell as an instructor. During the next five years she published nine papers on her research. Some people thought her research papers were brilliant, while others could not understand them. The papers were very complicated, even for other scientists and researchers.

In 1931, Barbara had to give up her position as instructor. Cornell did not give permanent teaching jobs to women, and it was not going to start with Barbara. Although Barbara was one of the leading scientists in her field, she could not get full-time work to continue her research.

Barbara used corn for most of her genetic research.

For the next few years, she struggled along with the help of small grants. Then, in 1936, friends found her a teaching position at the University of Missouri. This job was not a success. Barbara did not fit in. She shocked many of the professors by wearing pants, and she scared many of the students by her gruff manner. Again, the university refused to give her a permanent job because she was a woman.

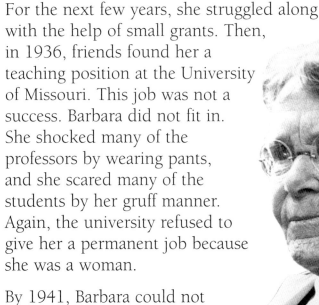

By 1941, Barbara could not stand the situation, and she walked out. She had no idea how she would earn her living, but she was determined to find a way to continue her research.

Quick Notes

- Barbara's theories were so complicated that they were very difficult to explain. This was one reason why they went unrecognized for so long. In 1951, when the great geneticist Alfred Sturtevant was asked about her "jumping gene" theory, he replied, "I didn't understand one word she said, but if she says it is so, it must be so."

- When the world at last realized Barbara's genius, she received many honors. Between 1980 and 1981, she received eight major awards. Three of them were given in one week.

Accomplishments

Barbara spent the summer of 1941 working with a friend at the Cold Spring Harbor Laboratory on Long Island, New York. Toward the end of the year, Barbara's position became permanent. The Carnegie Institution had offered to pay her salary. At last, she could concentrate entirely on her research.

Cold Spring Harbor was to be Barbara's home for more than forty years. She almost lived in her laboratory, often working late into the night. She even entertained friends there. Her tiny apartment across the road was used only for sleeping. Most of the other researchers wore jeans, and the atmosphere was very relaxed. It suited Barbara perfectly. Each summer, she grew corn—a whole field of it—and each winter, she studied the dried corncobs and did her experiments.

As part of her research, Barbara **cross-bred** the corn and noted the changes that occurred. By 1945, she was getting some very strange corn plants. She realized that this was the result of something that was happening to the chromosomes. But what exactly was happening, and why?

Barbara expected her students to be as dedicated to their work as she was to her own. Few could match her intensity.

It took Barbara six years to find out. Like everyone else at the time, she thought that genes were strung along a chromosome like pearls on a string, always staying in the same position. Her experiments suggested that this was not true. A gene could jump to another position on the chromosome, thus causing changes in the next generation of a plant or animal.

When Barbara announced her theory in 1951, many scientists thought she was crazy. There could be no such thing as "jumping genes," they said. Everyone knew that genes did not change position.

Barbara was very disappointed. She had made an exciting discovery, and people were not taking her seriously. Not until the 1970s did scientists begin to realize the truth of her findings— partly because they had stronger microscopes.

In 1983, more than forty years after Barbara had begun her experiments, she was awarded the Nobel Prize in medicine and **physiology**. She was pleased that her work was recognized at last, but she did not enjoy the publicity. Barbara had always been a loner, and she was happiest when she was in her laboratory. "I've had so much fun there," she said. Even when she was over eighty, she still put in long days in the laboratory.

BACKGROUNDER

The Nobel Prize

Barbara was listening to the radio one morning in October 1983 when she heard the announcer say that she had won the Nobel Prize in medicine and physiology. The Nobel committee called her work one of the "greatest discoveries of our time in genetics."

"I was startled when I found they didn't understand my work, didn't take it seriously. But I just knew I was right."

KEY EVENTS

1953 Earns a bachelor's degree from Howard University

1955 Earns a master's degree from Cornell University

1957 Begins teaching at Howard University

1958 Marries Harold Morrison

1964 Marriage ends in divorce

1965 Joins Random House as an editor

1969 Publishes her first book, *The Bluest Eye*

1973 Publishes *Sula*

1977 Publishes *Song of Solomon*

1981 Publishes *Tar Baby*

1987 Publishes *Beloved*

1988 Wins Pulitzer Prize for *Beloved*

1989 Appointed professor at Princeton University

1992 Publishes *Jazz*

1993 Receives Nobel Prize in literature

1998 Publishes *Paradise*

"I think long and hard about what my novels should do."

Toni Morrison

American Writer

Early Years

Toni grew up in a family of storytellers. Both her parents told wonderful stories, and so did her grandmother. Some of their tales were scary, but they were always thrilling, full of magic and strange adventures. Many were African-American folktales.

African-American music was also part of Toni's childhood. Her parents, George and Ramah Wofford, were from the American South. By the time Toni was born, they had moved to Lorain, Ohio, but they taught their children about southern culture.

Toni was always a good student. She graduated with honors from Lorain High School and enrolled at Howard University in 1950.

BACKGROUNDER

African-American Folklore

African-American folklore comes from many cultures. Some of the stories and traditions come from Africa. The culture of the Caribbean is also an important influence. Much of African-American culture developed during the years of slavery. African Americans made up songs and stories to help them forget their hard life. These influences have created a folklore that is rich in legends, music, dance, and tradition.

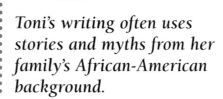

Toni's writing often uses stories and myths from her family's African-American background.

BACKGROUNDER

Racial Discrimination in the 1950s

Racism was more accepted in the 1950s than it is today, especially in the American South. The southern states had passed laws that did not allow African Americans to eat in most restaurants or travel in certain parts of trains or buses. Many places were for whites only. So were the best jobs. It was almost impossible for an African American to get a well-paid job or even a good education in the South. Although almost one hundred years had passed since slavery had been **abolished**, life had not improved much for thousands of African-American families in the southern states.

Toni did not begin to write until after she began teaching at Howard University in 1957.

Developing Skills

Toni studied English literature at Howard University, and in her spare time she joined the college theater group. The group toured the South each summer, and this gave Toni a chance to see the world her parents had described. She was delighted by the culture, but was disgusted by the **racism**.

In 1953, Toni graduated from Howard University and went to Cornell University to study for her master's degree. After getting her master's, she began a teaching career. She taught for two years at Texas Southern University and then moved back to Howard where she stayed for the next seven years.

Toni's years of teaching at Howard University changed her life because two important things happened. She met and married a Jamaican architect with whom she had two children, and she began to write.

Unlike most authors, Toni had not written stories when she was a child. She had been a reader rather than a writer. She might have stayed that way had she not joined a writers' group at Howard. The group met once a month, and all those attending had to bring something they had written.

One month, Toni worked on a story about a little black girl who wanted blue eyes. The story was really about racism. Toni was saying that black children should be proud of who they are. The story became the basis of her first book, *The Bluest Eye*, which was published in 1969.

By the time the book came out, Toni had left Howard University. She and her husband had divorced, and she had two sons to support. She worked as an editor for the well-known publishing company, Random House. This was a very busy time for her. After spending all day editing, she stayed up much of the night writing her next novel which she called *Sula*.

Sula is about an African-American woman who has far more confidence than the little girl who wanted blue eyes. Yet it, too, was about the racial problems faced by African Americans. Published in 1973, *Sula* was a great success and was nominated for the National Book Award. Although Toni had been writing for only ten years, she was already a famous author.

"When I finished [my first novel], I had all the permission I needed to become a writer. Someone who looked like me had written a masterpiece."

Quick Notes

- Toni has two sons, Harold and Slade.

- She has been a visiting professor at several universities.

- Toni was given the name Chloe by her parents. She changed it to Toni while she was at college.

Accomplishments

T oni suggested that Random House publish a book about African-American life. It should not be about politicians and leaders, she said. It should be about ordinary people, the type of people who usually get left out of history books.

The result was *The Black Book* which was published in 1974. Part scrapbook and part **anthology**, it included newspaper articles, letters, recipes, photos, and many other souvenirs. It gave a wonderful picture of African-American life during the past three hundred years.

The material in *The Black Book* inspired Toni to write more about African-American culture. She began to bring myths and legends into her stories. Her next book, *Song of Solomon*, was filled with songs and folklore. Called a masterpiece, it became an instant bestseller and won two major awards.

Song of Solomon sold more than three million copies and established Toni as a leading American writer. Since then, she has added to her reputation with each book. *Tar Baby* (1981) was another bestseller, and *Beloved* (1987) won numerous awards, including the Pulitzer Prize, one of the great honors in American literature.

Toni hoped that The Black Book *would highlight everyday heroes from African-American history.*

Jazz (1992) was another success. Then, in 1993, came the greatest success of all when Toni was awarded the Nobel Prize in literature. She was the first African-American woman to win the prize, and the first American woman to win it since Pearl Buck in 1938.

Several years passed before Toni's next novel, *Paradise*, was published in 1998. It is another powerful work. Toni has been called "one of our greatest writers" and "perhaps the finest novelist of our time."

As each novel increases Toni's reputation, she is showered with honors and awards. The honors are important, but even more important is the fact that Toni is sharing her culture with anyone who reads her books.

"I want my books to always be about something that is important to me."

Toni at a 1996 benefit performance with singer Jessye Norman.

BACKGROUNDER
Awards

Toni's books have won many awards. They include the National Book Award nomination and the Ohioana Book Award (for *Sula*); the National Book Critics Circle Award and the American Academy and Institute of Arts and Letters Award (for *Song of Solomon*); and the Pulitzer Prize, the Robert F. Kennedy Book Award, and the Melcher Book Award (for *Beloved*). In addition, in 1996 Toni was awarded the National Book Foundation Medal for Distinguished Contribution to American Letters.

Betty Williams (left) and
Mairead Corrigan, leaders
of the Northern Ireland Peace
Movement, standing beside
the wreckage of their car.
They were attacked by an
angry mob after attending
a peace rally.

Key Events

1976 Begin peace movement
1977 Awarded the Nobel
Peace Prize for 1976
1978 Resign from the
leadership of the peace
movement
1981 Mairead marries
Jack Maguire

1982 Betty marries her
second husband, James
Perkins
1994 Mairead protests
conditions in East Timor

Mairead Corrigan and Betty Williams

Irish Peace Activists

Early Years

Mairead and Betty were born in Belfast, the capital of Northern Ireland. Both were raised as Roman Catholics, and both attended Catholic schools. They did not know each other as children, but they had a lot in common.

Most of the Catholics in Belfast lived separately from the Protestants. Mairead's family lived in the Falls, a Catholic area in west Belfast. It was a very poor district, with run-down houses. Mairead left school when she was fourteen because her parents could not afford the fees. She worked in a factory for a few years and then found a job as a secretary.

Betty also lived in a Catholic area and also trained as a secretary. She married an English sailor and spent several years overseas before returning home. Although Betty's mother was Catholic, her father was Protestant, so she had friends from both religions. She hated to see Catholics and Protestants fighting in the streets of Belfast.

BACKGROUNDER

A Troubled Country

There has been fighting in Ireland since the twelfth century, when England first invaded the island. By the seventeenth century, all of Ireland was under British rule. After World War I, Britain agreed to grant self-government to most of Ireland. This happened in 1922 when the Irish Free State was formed from the twenty-six counties that were mainly Catholic. The remaining six counties, which were mainly Protestant and pro-British, stayed part of Britain and were renamed Northern Ireland. Today, the Free State is a separate country called the Republic of Ireland, and Northern Ireland is still part of the United Kingdom.

NORTHERN IRELAND

Irish Sea

REPUBLIC OF IRELAND

ENGLAND

BACKGROUNDER

Irish Catholics and Protestants

Religion in Ireland has divided the country into two opposing groups. Unlike England and Scotland, Ireland did not become Protestant during the sixteenth century. It stayed Catholic, but the invading English and Scots were Protestants. As the years passed, the Protestant settlers continued to think of themselves as British, but many Catholics did not. Most of the politicians and landowners were Protestant, which added to the problem. They made laws that favored their own group. The hatred between Catholics and Protestants grew more bitter each year. Britain hoped to solve the problem in 1922 when it set up the Irish Free State for the Catholics. But there were some Catholics living in Northern Ireland. By the 1960s, they were one-third of the population, yet Northern Ireland was still controlled by Protestants. This led to more bitterness and violence between Catholics and Protestants.

Developing Skills

The fighting in Ireland had become much worse during the years Betty and Mairead were growing up. Some people's homes were burned to the ground, and many people—both Catholic and Protestant—were killed. On the Catholic side, the violence was led by a secret organization called the Irish Republican Army (IRA). The main Protestant group was the Ulster Defense League.

Things became so bad in the late 1960s that Britain sent soldiers to keep peace and order. The British soldiers were not meant to take sides, but they often supported the Protestants. This was because many Catholics thought of the soldiers as enemies. Both Mairead and Betty had seen soldiers beating up Catholic children who had shouted or thrown stones at them.

Mairead was afraid of the soldiers, but she did not hate Protestants. Since the age of fourteen, she had belonged to a Catholic group that helped others. This brought her into contact with Protestants who were doing the same work. Betty, too, was working for a group run by a Protestant minister who was trying to bring Catholics and Protestants together.

"Young men and boys of my area were becoming violent, aggressive, almost murderers; and they were becoming heroes in the community."

Betty Williams

Both Mairead and Betty wished the fighting would stop, but they did not think they could do much about it. They expected others to take the lead.

Their attitudes changed on August 10, 1976. On that day, Mairead's sister Anne was out for a walk with three of her children. An escaping IRA car, whose driver was shot dead at the wheel by British soldiers, crashed into them. All three children were killed, and their mother was seriously injured. Mairead went on television to beg for an end to violence and to condemn the IRA. This caused a great stir, because Catholics did not normally speak against the IRA.

The accident had also affected Betty. She had been there when it happened and had watched in horror as the car hit the children. She decided to go from door to door asking people to sign a petition supporting an end to the violence.

After two days, Betty had collected more than six thousand signatures on her petition which she read on television. When Mairead heard of her efforts, she invited Betty to the children's funeral. The two women met and decided they would do everything they could to bring peace to Northern Ireland.

Mairead has said that she would risk her life to bring peace to her country.

Accomplishments

B etty and Mairead formed a group called Women for Peace that they later renamed Community for Peace People. Within two weeks, they had thirty thousand followers—Protestants as well as Catholics. They organized peace rallies and marches, gathering more followers each day. At one of their rallies, hundreds of Catholic women from the Falls walked to Shankill Road, a Protestant area, and were welcomed by the women who lived there.

Before long, the movement spread throughout Northern Ireland. Most people were tired of the fighting. Yet it could not be stopped easily. The **extremists** on both sides did not want to lay down their guns and mistrusted any moves toward peace.

Quick Notes

- **Betty eventually moved to the United States.**

- **Between 1969 and 1975, over fourteen hundred people were injured or killed in Ireland due to the troubles. By 1977, the killings had decreased by half.**

In October 1976, Betty and Mairead visited the United States to ask Irish Americans to stop sending money to the IRA and other extremist groups. The money was spent on weapons, they said. Many Americans responded by donating money to the peace movement. There was similar support from Canada, Mexico, Europe, and many other places.

Betty and Mairead read some of the hundreds of telegrams they received at a "Women for Peace" rally.

Within only a few months, Betty and Mairead had become famous. Their efforts to bring Catholics and Protestants together won them the Nobel Peace Prize in 1977.

Even so, their country's problems were not over. When Mairead and Betty asked the extremist groups to hand in their weapons, both sides refused. The two women were called traitors, and their lives were threatened. At one meeting, they were beaten and had to escape to a church.

In the years since then, Mairead and Betty have continued to work for peace, although they retired from the leadership of their movement in 1978. Meanwhile, many Irish Protestants and Catholics have been working to end the conflict. In the 1990s, there have been long periods without fighting, and peace plans have been discussed. This is partly because of the movement that Betty and Mairead started more than twenty years ago.

In 1993, Mairead and Betty went on a peace mission to Bangkok, Thailand, with a number of other Nobel Peace Prize winners. Betty and Mairead are in the back row beginning at the far left. South Africa's Desmond Tutu stands in center of the back row and Tibet's Dalai Lama is seated on the far right.

BACKGROUNDER
Steps toward Peace

In September 1994, the IRA and most of the Protestant groups agreed to stop fighting. The peace lasted for a year and a half. During this time, talks were held to try to solve Northern Ireland's problems in a way that would please all parties. However, in February 1996, violence started again. Nevertheless, the efforts toward peace continued, and new talks began in September 1997. This was a great step forward because it was the first time that members of all the different groups had agreed to sit down together to discuss peace.

More Women in Profile

The following pages list a few more women Nobel Prize winners you may want to read about on your own. Use the Suggested Reading list to learn about these and other Nobel Prize winners.

1860–1935

Laura Jane Addams

American Social Worker

Laura began her work in Chicago, where she founded a community shelter called Hull House. During World War I, she formed the Woman's Peace Party to try to stop the fighting. She continued to work for world peace after the war and was awarded the Nobel Peace Prize in 1931. Laura and a fellow American, Nicholas Butler, shared the prize. When giving her the prize, the Nobel committee noted that they were paying "homage to the work which women can do for the cause of peace … among nations."

Laura Jane Addams

1867–1961

Emily Greene Balch

American Peace Activist

Emily campaigned for peace during World War I, and she founded the Women's International League for Peace and Freedom. In 1919, she lost her job as a college teacher because of her **pacifist** views. Emily received the Nobel Peace Prize in 1946.

1896–1957

Gerty Radnitz Cori

Czechoslovakian Biochemist

Gerty and her husband, Carl Cori, received the Nobel Prize in medicine and **physiology** in 1947. The couple discovered how an animal's body changes starch in its tissues into usable sugar.

1918–

Gertrude Elion

American Biochemist

As a researcher for drug companies, Gertrude developed drugs to treat diseases such as cancer and **malaria**. She was awarded the Nobel Prize in medicine and **physiology** in 1988 with her fellow researcher Herbert Hitchings.

1906–1972

Maria Goeppert-Mayer

German Physicist

Like many women scientists, Maria's work was often ignored. Some scientists had never heard of her discoveries and were surprised when she won the Nobel Prize. She was awarded the Nobel Prize in **physics** with Hans Jensen in 1963 for their study of the structure of the **atom**. During World War II, she was part of the team of scientists that developed the atomic bomb.

Maria Goeppert-Mayer

1910–1994

Dorothy Crowfoot Hodgkin

English Chemist and Crystallographer

Dorothy was awarded the Nobel Prize in **chemistry** in 1964 for her study of the chemical structure of Vitamin B12. This work has made it possible to treat pernicious anemia, a lack of red blood cells in the body. She was also the first person to use the computer to detail the structure of **penicillin**.

1897–1956

Irène Joliot-Curie

French Radiochemist

The daughter of scientists Marie and Pierre Curie, Irène followed in her parents' footsteps. She married a fellow researcher, Frédéric Joliot, and together they carried on her parents' study of radioactivity. Irène and Frédéric were awarded the Nobel Prize in **chemistry** in 1935. The couple worked to develop atomic energy in France and worked for the World Peace Movement.

1909–

Rita Levi-Montalcini

Italian Neuroembryologist

In 1986, Rita was awarded the Nobel Prize in medicine and **physiology** for her important discoveries about the way nerve cells grow. She shared the prize with Stanley Cohen, the biochemist who had worked with her on the research. Rita is Jewish, and during World War II, she secretly set up a laboratory in her home because the Italian government forbade Jews to practice medicine or science. After the war, she moved to the United States where she did much of her groundbreaking research. She later returned to Italy.

1889–1957

Gabriela Mistral

Chilean Poet

Gabriela was awarded the Nobel Prize in literature in 1945 for her powerful poetry. Her name was a symbol for Latin America's hopes for the future. Gabriela used her personal feelings of love and grief to write poetry many people understood. As well as writing beautiful poetry, Gabriela worked for better education in Chile. She also served as a Chilean diplomat in several countries.

Gabriela Mistral

1891–1970

Leonie Nelly Sachs

German Writer and Holocaust Survivor

Of Jewish ancestry, Leonie wrote plays, poems, and stories about the terrible things that had been done to the Jews, especially during World War II. She was awarded the Nobel Prize in literature in 1966. The main theme in all her work is human suffering, but she believed strongly in the power of forgiveness and hope.

1843–1914

Bertha von Suttner

Austrian Author and Pacifist

Bertha formed the Austrian Peace Society and worked for the peace movement. She wrote several novels about the horrors of war, including the best-selling *Lay Down Your Arms* (1889). Her novel showed the brutality of war rather than its glory or heroism. Bertha was also the editor of a **pacifist** journal. In 1905, she was the first woman to be awarded the Nobel Peace Prize. Bertha had been friends with Alfred Nobel, and it was partly due to her influence that he established the peace prize in his will.

Jody Williams

1950–

Jody Williams

American Anti-war Activist

Jody has long been an activist against war. She spent several years in El Salvador, arranging medical care for children who had been hurt during the civil war. Jody was awarded the Nobel Peace Prize in 1997. The prize was shared by Jody and the International Campaign to Ban Landmines which she started in 1991. The Nobel committee said that, because of Jody's efforts, a ban on landmines was no longer just a hopeful dream.

1910–1997

Mother Teresa

Yugoslavian Missionary Nun

Born Agnes Gonxha Bojaxhiu, Mother Teresa devoted her life to the poor and dying. When she was a young woman, she went to India as a Roman Catholic **missionary**. She soon realized that her work was most needed in the **slums**. In 1950, she founded the Missionaries of Charity to help the homeless and dying in Calcutta. Over the years, she set up more than fifty schools, orphanages, and houses for the poor in India and many other countries. Because she did so much for the poor, she was known as the Saint of the Gutters. Mother Teresa was awarded the Nobel Peace Prize in 1979.

1921–

Rosalyn Sussman Yalow

American Medical Physicist

Rosalyn developed a way of measuring levels of **insulin** and **hormones** in the blood. Her work has been especially helpful in treating diabetes, a disease in which too much sugar is found in the blood. She was awarded the Nobel Prize in medicine and **physiology** in 1977.

Glossary

abolish: to get rid of a law, institution, or custom

anthology: a collection of poems or stories

assassinate: to murder someone, especially a politically important person

atom: the smallest part of an element that has all the properties of the element

bigotry: when a person sticks to an opinion without considering any other ideas

biology: the study of living things

calorie: a unit used to measure heat

characteristic: an individual feature

chemistry: the study of elements

cross-breed: to breed different kinds of plants or animals to create new plants or animals

democracy: a government in which the people vote for their leaders

economics: the study of the production, distribution, and use of money and goods

extremist: a person who acts drastically

hormone: a substance in the body that influences the activities of certain organs

independence: freedom from control by another person or country

insulin: a hormone in the body that helps it digest sugar

malaria: a fever that is spread by mosquitoes

missionary: a person who goes to another country to preach religion or bring medical help

pacifist: a person who believes that war should be abolished

penicillin: an antibiotic drug used to treat certain infections

physics: a science that studies matter, heat, light, and sound

physiology: the study of living things, their parts, and their functions

racism: discrimination against people because of their race

radiation: a form of energy that includes light, heat, and X-rays

radioactive: giving off radiation

radiation sickness: a disease resulting from too much exposure to radiation

rebel: to refuse to obey someone in authority, especially a government

slum: an area of a city that is crowded, poor, and unclean

species: types of plants and animals

Suggested Reading

Aaseng, Nathan. *The Peace Seekers: The Nobel Peace Prize*. Minneapolis: Lerner, 1987.

Fisher, Leonard E. *Marie Curie*. New York: Macmillan, 1994.

Forbes, Malcolm and Jeff Bloch. *Women Who Made a Difference*. New York: Simon & Schuster, 1990.

Johnson, Linda C. *Mother Teresa: Protector of the Sick*. New York: Blackbirch Press, 1991.

Keller, Gail E. *Jane Addams*. New York: Crowell, 1971.

McGravne, Sharon Bertsch. *Nobel Prize Winners in Science*. New York: Carol Publishing Group, 1993.

Meyer, Edith P. *In Search of Peace: Winners of the Nobel Peace Prize, 1901–75*. Nashville: Abingdon Press, 1978.

Nobel Prize Winners. 1987-1991 Supplement. New York: H. W. Wilson Co., 1992.

Raven, Susan and Alison Weir. *Women of Achievement*. New York: Harmony Books, 1981.

Saari, Peggy. *Prominent Women of the 20th Century*. Detroit: UXL, 1986.

The Who's Who of Nobel Prize Winners, 1901–90. Phoenix, Arizona: Oryx, 1991.

Thompson, Clifford. *Nobel Prize Winners. Supplement, 1992-1996*. New York: H. W. Wilson Co., 1997.

Wasson, Tyler. *Nobel Prize Winners*. New York: H. W. Wilson Co., 1981.

Index

apartheid 20, 21, 23
Aung San, General 7

Booker Prize 23
Buddhism 11
Burma (Myanmar) 6, 7, 8, 9-11

censorship 22
chromosomes 26, 28, 29
Curie, Pierre 12, 15-17

genetics 26, 29

International Campaign to Ban
    Landmines 45
Ireland 37-41
Irish Republican Army (IRA) 38,
    41

Joliot-Curie, Irène 15, 17, 43
jumping gene theory 28, 29

Mandela, Nelson 23
Missionaries of Charity 45

National Book Award 33, 35
Nobel, Alfred 4, 44

Nobel Peace Prize 4, 6, 11, 23,
    36, 41, 42, 44, 45
Nobel Prize in chemistry 4, 12,
    17, 43
Nobel Prize in literature 4, 18, 23,
    30, 35, 44
Nobel Prize in medicine and
    physiology 4, 24, 29, 42, 43, 45
Nobel Prize in physics 4, 5, 12,
    17, 43
Northern Ireland 37-39, 40

pacifist 4, 42
Poland 13, 17
polonium 12, 15, 16, 17
Pulitzer Prize 30, 34, 35

radiation 15, 16, 17
radium 12, 15, 16, 17
racism 32

South Africa 19-23

Tutu, Desmond 23, 41

Ulster Defense League 38

Women for Peace 40

1 2 3 4 5 6 7 8 9 0 Printed in Canada 7 6 5 4 3 2 1 0 9 8